Diary of a Sleepless Dreamer

A Poetry Collection

Hanna Brooke

Diary of a Sleepless Dreamer copyright © 2024 by Hanna Brooke. All rights reserved. No part of this book may be used or reproduced in any manner whatsoever without written permission, except in the case of brief quotations embodied in critical articles and reviews.

Printed in the United States of America.

Cover design by Breanna Lunsford.

ISBN: 979-8-322-676379

In memory of Kristina, "Tonnie", and Larry...

The ones who always believed in me

Table of Contents

Introduction..6

Section I: Dreams..8

Section II: Struggles..26

Section III: Loss...58

Section IV: Love (But Mostly Heartbreak) 72

Section V: Trauma...100

Section VI: Growth..124

Section VII: Faith...150

Introduction

This book is for the dreamers and the broken-hearted. This book is for survivors with loved ones departed. This book is for those without the prettiest past. This book is for those who had to grow up too fast.

This book is for those with traumas, unspoken. This book is for those who've had promises broken. This book is for those still feeling the burn. This book is for those with no way to turn. This book is for those still making it through. If this sounds familiar, this book is for you.

Section I: Dreams

Dreamer

I may be an insomniac

But that doesn't mean I'm not a dreamer

So when I can't sleep

I dream of grass that is greener

I dream of the life I would like to create

I dream of not having so much on my plate

I dream of a day that I can awake

Without feeling like life is too much to take

Impossible To Sleep

At night, my mind is an endless sea of ideas—ideas about all sorts of things. I try to close my eyes and tell myself not to think, but it never seems to work. It's impossible to sleep...so I dream with my eyes wide open.

Open Your Eyes

They say "the eyes are the windows to the soul"

But what if my eyes are just here to fill my skull?

They say that "beauty is in the eye of the beholder"

But if that were true, what are these lies that they've told her?

They say that "real eyes realize real lies"

But sometimes these lies are dressed in disguise

They say that "eyes have a language of their own"

But how can we speak in the absence of tone?

They say that our "eyes say what words can't"

But my eyes can't speak what I'm here to rant.

They say to "cross your heart and hope to die"

To "stick a needle in your eye"

To make a promise you'll forever keep

Even when you're gone and buried deep...

But what if that promise ends up broken

And you cannot fix the wound you've opened?

They say to "close your eyes and make a wish"

But what if your penny gets swallowed by a fish?

They say to "believe with your eyes, not your ears"

But everything isn't always as it appears.

So what is the point of the words that I've spoken?

To tell you that you can dream with your eyes wide open

So don't let your dreams end the second you've awoken

Now read it again, and let it all soak in.

Music Must Be Magic

Music must be magic

It transports me back in time

To memories I've long forgotten

Buried deep within my mind

This Pen

I have a belief

And you may think it's crazy

But I truly believe

I can change the world with this pen

One Team

It seems like every day, I hear about oppression

And honestly, it's starting to cause me depression

Everyone just wants to be heard and seen

But some people choose to be flat-out mean

In the end, people walk all over others

Not caring that we're all sisters and brothers

I guess it's just a childish dream

To wish that we were on one team

Wicked Whispers

Wicked whispers in my ear

Make it hard to think

Wicked whispers in my ear

Saying I will sink

Wicked whispers in my ear

But I call their bluff

Wicked whispers I can't hear

If I dream loud enough

Open-Minded

To have an open mind

And put the past behind

To think for yourself

And not impose on someone else

To agree to disagree

We can unite humanity

If I Were Not Afraid

All the things I'd change

If I were not afraid

To be the person I want to be

Without pretending

All the things I'd do

If I were not afraid

Of being approached by a stranger

With ill intention

All the things I'd say

If I were not afraid

To speak what's on my mind

Without fear of confrontation

Midnight Miracles

Am I the only one who has all the motivation in the world at night, and none during the day? Sometimes I wonder just how much change I could make in my life if I were only this energized in the daytime. In the morning, I am utterly useless. But at night? I could almost make miracles happen.

Black and White

Life is not black and white

With solid, clear-cut lines

Life is more than wrong or right

That society defines

If I Had Wings

If I had wings

All the places I would go

If I had wings

I could see all things below

If I had wings

I could fly right through the clouds

If I had wings

I would avoid all of the crowds

If I had wings

I wouldn't have to wait

If I had wings

I would never be late

If I had wings

I would soar through the trees

If I had wings

Life would be a breeze

A Poet Like You

I'm a poet like my mother

Who wrote about life

I'm a poet like my brother

Who writes about strife

I was born with poetry

Written on my heart

Poetry has always been

My family's art

1 O'clock

1:00am

I can't sleep

Sitting here

Counting sheep

2:00am

Still not tired

Why do I

Feel so wired?

3:00am

Still awake

How much longer

Will it take?

4:00am

I need rest

But it's hard

When I'm stressed

5:00am

Still in bed

I can hardly

Lift my head

6:00am

I see the sun

Now it's time

To sleep 'til one

Section II: Struggles

Going Through It

There are days that I feel invincible

The next day, I can't do something simple

It's like I'm stuck standing on the bottom step

Sinking deeper and deeper into the ocean's depth

I try to swim up, I try to breathe

But no matter what, I'm stuck beneath

Another wave, another bill to pay

But it's alright

It'll be okay

Panic Button

I wish I had a button

That I could choose to press

When I start to panic

To relieve me from my stress

Making Choices

I'm not good at making choices

Because no matter what I pick

I can't help but wonder

Should I have chosen differently?

Pages of Poetry

I pour my pain out into pages of poetry.

Without writing, where would I be?

Sober and Hungover

Close all the curtains

Block out the light

Everything around me

Seems way too bright

Turn down the volume

So I cannot hear

Everything around me

So loud and clear

There's ringing in my ears

And the room won't be still

It's swirling and spinning

And making me ill

You may not believe me

But I am quite sober

So why does it feel like

I'm completely hungover?

Broken Compass

Can a broken compass lead me home?

Or will I end up lost and alone?

When the Party Ends

When the party is over

And everyone's gone home

I can't help but feeling

Like I'm utterly alone

All My Mistakes

All of my mistakes

Weigh upon my mind

And when I get ahead

They pull me back behind

Drained, yet Drowning

Can you drown in an empty lake?

Am I asleep or am I awake?

Is this real or is this fake?

How much more can I take?

I am drowning, yet I am drained.

That is what I need explained.

I keep trying to rack my brain,

But it's driving me insane.

If my tub is empty, then why am I sinking?

It feels like it's pouring, but it's only sprinkling.

If my tub is empty, then why am I wrinkling?

Someone help me to quit overthinking.

All the Rage

I have spies watching me

Snooping through my page

Nosey people everywhere

I guess I'm all the rage

Ticking Timer

There's a ticking timer

In my head

That will not stop

Until I'm dead

The ticking timer

Counts each day

And won't rewind

Or go away

Brain Fog

It's foggy in my brain today

There's a mist masking my mind

Brain fog makes my mind delay

I keep falling behind

Low Battery

Put me on the charger

And leave me for the night

Put me on the charger

So I can feel alright

Put me on the charger

So I can face the day

Put me on the charger

So I will be okay

Put me on the charger

And leave me there, wired

Put me on the charger

So I won't be this tired

Pain, Pain

Pain, Pain,

Go away

I can't deal with you today

Pain, Pain,

Don't come back

I can't take one more attack

Writer's Block

I think that I have "writer's block"

In my mind, there is a lock

That's keeping me from creating

So I sit here, simply waiting

Nightmares

I am afraid that if I go to bed

It'll release all the monsters trapped in my head

When I awake, I am covered in sweat

I try to sleep, but it's hard to forget

Underwater

When I go underwater

The sounds all finally cease

When I go underwater

I finally feel at peace

Hiding in My Hoodie

I pull my hoodie closed

When the sun shines its light

Or it feels way too bright

And I'm not alright

I pull my hoodie closed

When I'm stuck in a crowd

Or the people are too loud

And I can't stand the sound

I pull my hoodie closed

When my energy is gone

Or the lights are left on

And I feel withdrawn

I pull my hoodie closed

When I have just cried

Or I want to hide

What I'm feeling inside

Uncomfortable

My jeans feel too tight

My hair isn't right

I don't like the light

Am I too uptight?

Mirror, Mirror

Mirror, Mirror

On the wall

I'm not the fairest

Of them all

I'm not thin

Or super tall

But I am real

I'm not a doll

Fight-or-Flight

When you are under attack

Your mind and body will react

Fight-or-flight, they have to choose

Once they do, they light a fuse

Adrenaline floods your brain

So that you are free from pain

This response is expected

When a danger is detected

But if the fuse remains lit

Constantly and doesn't quit

If it stays activated

By a threat you created

Your body will not function right

And you'll be stuck in fight-or-flight

Inhaler

Like an inhaler, counting each breath

Each day is numbered until your death

So don't let your time go to waste

A wasted life can't be replaced

Creamy Coffee

Creamy coffee in my cup

Brewed at morning's peak

Creamy coffee, wake me up

So I won't fall asleep

Perfect Pill

I wish there was a perfect pill

That would release my stress

I'd pop it in and wait until

I finally felt my best

Bullying Myself

I call myself lazy

Because I can't move from my bed

I call myself crazy

Because I'm stuck inside my head

I call myself worthless

Because that's how I feel

But bullying myself

Won't help me to heal

Mind Mechanic

I need a mind mechanic

To fix my broken parts

I need a tune-up and alignment

And an engine that will start

I need a mind mechanic

Who can tell me what is wrong

I need a mind mechanic

So my engine can run strong

Over and Over

Over and over again

I find myself back where I started

Feeling like I haven't made an ounce of progress

But maybe that's because

I keep moving the finish line

Liar, Liar

My mind is a liar

That tells me I am worthless

And that I'll never accomplish my dreams

My mind is a bully

That takes away my confidence

By telling me that

I'll never be enough

Recipe for Poetry

The recipe for poetry comes straight from the heart. Must a poet be tortured to create a work of art?

Section III: Loss

A Different Life for Us

Sometimes I imagine

A different life we'd live

And in that life I'd give you

All the love that I could give

Sometimes I imagine

That you never went away

And sometimes I just wish that

My tears could make you stay

I wish that all my wishing

Wasn't wasted pennies in a well

I wish that I knew magic

So I could do a simple spell

Sometimes I imagine

Telling you about my life

And sometimes I just wish that

You could give me some advice

I'd let you know how much I've grown

And everything I've done

Catching up on things you've missed

Hours past the sun

I wish that you were here right now

So I could let you know

That no matter what I do

I just can't let you go

I want to make you dinner

And tell you about my day

And give you some grandchildren

When all your hair turns gray

I know that life can change

And that some things don't last

But even when I know these things

My heart looks to the past

You were here and then you weren't

And I never said goodbye

I guess what I am saying is

I wish you didn't die

Gone

Sometimes death is slow

And in these times we know

Before it's time to go

But sometimes death is fast

We don't know before they pass

That the moment is the last

Singing to Your Grave

If I could sing a song

That would reach your ear

I'd sing it loud and strong

Hoping you would hear

If I could sing a song

That would bring you back

I'd sing it all day long

'til my voice would crack

When I Look in the Mirror

When I look in the mirror

I see my mother's face

But when I look a little clearer

It's me that's in her place

I Saw You Today

I saw you today

The person I once knew

I saw you today

But was it really you?

My eyes lit up

And my heart began to race

But when I looked a little closer

It was someone else's face

I missed you today

My mother and my friend

I missed you today

And I will until the end

Last Goodbye

I didn't know that you would die

So soon after that day

If I could have a last goodbye

I know just what I'd say

Ticket Back in Time

If I could buy a ticket

To go explore my mind

I'd hop right in my seat

And quickly press rewind

I'd go back to a better time

Before you passed away

I'd watch all our memories

And then I'd press replay

Wasted Wishes

Wasted wishes in a well

At least I can say I tried

Wasted wishes in a well

Can't fix someone who died

First Experience of Loss

I had a "stick buddy" when I was a child

I found it out where the flowers grew wild

That stick was my only friend

Until it met its brutal end

Because I used it to hit his calf,

My brother cracked stick buddy in half

I cried and cried and no one knew why

My grandma gave me some tape to try

But the tape just wouldn't stick

My buddy was broken

He couldn't be fixed

That Beautiful

When I was a kid

I'd look at my mom

And hope that one day

I'd grow up to be that beautiful

Section IV: Love (But Mostly Heartbreak)

Haunted Heart

If I told you how I really feel

Do you think my heart would finally heal

If I got it off my chest

Would I finally get some rest

I keep thinking about you

And all the things we used to do

You're all I've ever wanted

But now my heart is fucking haunted

By memories of what we used to be

Replaying all the things I used to see

The secrets that I'll always keep

Maybe tonight, I'll get some sleep

Sore

I thought it was different than before

Never knew love could leave my heart this sore

Love

Why does some love cause so much hate?

Some people don't believe that love is up to fate.

But most of the time, when two hearts meld into one,

It happens before we even know it's begun.

When it comes to love, we are not making a decision—

There's an unknown force controlling this collision.

Some call it "destiny", some call it "Cupid",

But no matter who you love, that love isn't stupid.

Who's To Say?

Who's to say where the horizon begins and ends?

Who's to say where a rainbow begins to bend?

Who's to say when my heart should start to mend?

Feelings vs. Love

FEELINGS FADE
FEELINGS FAD
FEELINGS FA
FEELINGS F
FEELINGS
FEELING
FEELIN
FEELI
FEEL
FEE
FE
F

L
LO
LOV
LOVE
LOVE L
LOVE LA
LOVE LAS
LOVE LAST
LOVE LASTS

Something's Wrong

You don't see me standing there

You don't feel me, you don't care

Something's different in the air

You don't think that something's wrong

It's been this way far too long

I don't feel like I belong

Still Beating

My heart has been broken

By hurtful words that were spoken

In it, feelings have awoken

My heart has been shot

After I pleaded and fought

For someone I loved a lot

But the worst feeling won't fade

In my mind, it has replayed

From the day I was betrayed

I was bleeding in black

It was more than just a crack

A knife in the back

I tried to be tough

But I felt really rough

Like I wasn't quite enough

But these feelings, I'm defeating

And although I'm still bleeding

My heart is broken, but beating

~~Loving~~ Leaving You

Loving you was easy

But leaving you has been the hardest thing I've ever done

Move On

How can I move on

From these painful memories

When everything reminds me

Of the way it used to be?

Shaken Bottle

My heart was very vulnerable,

So I decided to protect it.

But despite my attempts,

It was harmed.

This time, I decided to double my guard,

Ensuring that my heart would not suffer again.

But once again, my heart was hurt.

Third times the charm.

I wrapped my heart in a security blanket,

Protecting it so that no one could hurt me again—

Distracting myself from the pain,

Turning off my emotions,

Burying them deep within me.

Seldom now I think of the pain,

But when I do, it all comes rushing back.

Like a bottle of soda dropped on the floor,

The pain comes spewing from my heart.

I try to put the top back on,

But it's too late.

The contents have escaped.

But in the end, the bottle is a little emptier.

It's hard to forget…

Cheap Love

Cheap love isn't worth your time

And costs more than you think

Cheap love takes your every dime

And causes you to sink

Falling for You

            I
        A
    M
            F
                A
            L
                L
                    I
            N
        G

            F
        O
    R

            Y
                O
                U

Lock and Key

You could hurt me a million times

You could commit a million crimes

But one look in your eyes

And I'll forget all your lies

I guarded my heart like a top-notch prison

But you came along, and my hopes were risen

I jumped at the thought that somebody cared

To believe someone loved me, I was scared

You made me feel loved and free inside

But every day at the ocean ends with the tide

You were just lonely and needed a friend

I was still healing, my heart on the mend

Everyone knows how fairytales go

"Happily Ever After"—no feelings of woe

But what they don't tell you

What your eyes couldn't see

Is that there's no turning back

Once you give them that key

Find Your Way

Don't go looking for reasons to stay

If you do, there's a price to pay

When it's time, please don't delay

In the end, you'll find your way

Measuring Mistakes

Can a clock count the hours that I've wasted on you?

Or measure the moment that you broke my heart in two?

Would a ruler reflect our distance apart?

Could a scale score the heaviness of my heart?

And what is the weight on my shoulders, I wonder?

Would a barometer break from the pressure I'm under?

Could the heat of the moment be taken with a thermometer?

Could I speed up my healing if I used a speedometer?

Could a level let me level with you and get everything straight?

Can a compass come correct the direction of my fate?

Indifferent

Maybe there will be a day when I wake up, and you aren't the first person on my mind.

And maybe one day when I think about you, I won't feel sad or jealous or broken, but indifferent.

The Face of My Forever

When this began, it felt like a hopeless endeavor

But now I'm staring in the face of my forever

Shattered

Shattered pieces on the floor

I don't even recognize anymore

I pick up each piece and wipe off the stains

I wipe off any feeling for you that remains

Sorting and shifting the pieces around

Slowly, the mystery is unwound

These were the pieces that once formed my heart

They were there before you tore them apart

Broken, black, and bleeding in vain

I don't think my heart could take any more pain

Slipping right through your fingertips

Breaking beyond the repair of your lips

An empty hole rests in my chest

I'm past the point of feeling depressed

Protect your heart, never give it away

Otherwise, it's a steep price to pay

I grab another piece and find it its spot

Grabbing and gluing and fixing a lot

Fixing my heart cause no one else will

Beginning to recognize it before it was ill

I pick up my heart and put it back in its place

Very carefully, not in a haste

I breathe again, all on my own

Finally okay with being alone

Broken Without You

Can't we go back to the day

Before you took your love away

Maybe I lived a lie

But at least back then I didn't cry

Myself to sleep each night

Hoping that you might

Still love me deep down

Your love was my crown

Over wasn't real

Broken hearts would always heal

But that isn't true

And I'm broken without you

One Call Away

When you feel all alone

I'll pick up the phone

If you had a bad day

I'm one call away

Buy Your Love

If I could buy your love

Would I even want it?

What would it be worth

If I didn't earn it?

If I could buy your love

What would be the cost?

If I could buy your love

Could it still be lost?

A Band-Aid for My Broken Heart

There aren't Band-Aids that can fix broken hearts

Or stitches to keep them from falling apart

There's no surgery to repair broken trust

Or a doctor to treat a soul that's crushed

But if there were that kind of doctor

I'd sign up and take that offer

Section V: Trauma

Play "House"

When I was a kid

I loved to play "house"

I would be the mom

And I would have a spouse

And things were as perfect

As they could be

Like I wished they had been

In my real family

'Cause when I played house

Both parents were there

And dad didn't scream

And pull out mom's hair

When I played house

Dad wasn't in jail

And he could just speak

Without sending me mail

And when I played house

Mom didn't cry

Worrying and stressing

About how we'd get by

And now that I look back

I can't help but see

That that was the way

I wished things could be

Life's a Lesson

Life's a series of lessons

That I didn't study for...

The hardest one I learned

Was not to trust you anymore.

Dark Memories

I have dark memories

Floating in my head

That I'll never forget

Even when I'm dead

I have dark memories

That I cannot shake

No matter what I try

I cannot escape

Skeletons in My Closet

The skeletons in my closet

Sit there sipping tea

Waiting on the day that

I finally set them free

Draw the Line

Let's draw the line here

With a stick in the sand

To never again cross

Into forbidden land

Let's draw the line here

And go our separate ways

And never again speak

For the rest of our days

You broke my trust

And now you are banned

Let's draw the line here

With a stick in the sand

Waiting for Silence

I cover my ears

So I can't hear the violence

While I sit in my room

Waiting for the silence

Grow Up Fast

I had to grow up fast

Because of the cards that I was dealt

So I made myself be strong

Since I had to raise myself

I buried all my feelings

And I pushed people away

I was fiercely independent

And I still am to this day

I had to grow up fast

Because of the cards that I was dealt

So I'm still learning how to trust

And not rely just on myself

What Happens?

What happens when I get pushed too far?

What happens when it becomes more than I can take?

What happens when you hurt me again?

What happens when I finally break?

Pass Your Inspection

If I could pass your inspection

And remove my every defect

Maybe then we could form a connection

And put an end to my neglect

If I could achieve perfection

And always be correct

Maybe then I could feel your affection

Or at least have your respect

If I could end the rejection

Or learn to just deflect

Maybe that would be the exception

But that I don't expect

Rough Draft: Story of My Life

I've been rewriting the same story my whole life

Trying to predict the ending

Forgetting to enjoy the present

Constantly reliving the past

Brainwashed

Have you ever been brainwashed?

Well I guess you wouldn't know...

Unless it was over

Or someone told you so.

Brooke

There was a young girl

(We'll call her Brooke)

Who was the daughter of

A liar and a crook

From a young age

She felt all alone

But she hid it so well

You wouldn't have known

She tried to be kind

She tried to fit in

But her heart was shut off

It wouldn't open

She moved all around

So how could you blame her

No matter where she went

No one would claim her

After a while

She began to lose hope

So she turned to her journal

In an effort to cope

There was a young girl

But her name wasn't Brooke

I am that girl

And this is my book

Buried Treasure

Something's hidden

Very deep

Like a secret

Hard to keep

Buried treasure

In the ground

Will not rest 'til

It is found

Unsaid

They say some things are better left unsaid

So we carry our secrets until we are dead

I zip my lips and throw away the key

Like a message in a bottle lost at sea

Carrying the burden upon my back

Almost like an unspoken pact

Fearing that if I ever speak

Everyone will think I'm weak

Tricky Trauma

Tricky trauma tells me that

I am not okay

Tricky trauma makes me feel

Like I can't face the day

Tricky trauma takes me back

To a hurtful place

Tricky trauma doesn't want

Me to have my space

Disappeared

You looked me in the face

And called me a disgrace

You saw that I was low

And dealt a fatal blow

You became someone I feared

And wondered why I disappeared

The Leaf That Left

There are broken branches in my family tree

There are twisted twigs that only I can see

There's rotten wood creeping up the base

There's mold and moss all over the place

There are a few lost leaves lying on the ground

And that is where I can be found

I Am Free

You took away my choice

And treated me like dirt

You silenced my voice

And asked why I was hurt

You spun lies about me

To make me look bad

But now that I am free

You're the one who's sad

Stood My Ground

You bury me with dirt

Lightning hits the ground

I feel so sad and hurt

Rainwater all around

Left alone to die

With insects in my grave

I can't help but cry

I'm too far gone to save

The sun begins to shine

And my leaves begin to sprout

I will be just fine

There was no need to doubt

You buried me with dirt

And lightning struck around

But I took all of the hurt

And I still stood my ground

Pretty Pictures

Pretty pictures on the wall

Telling them a lie

Pretty pictures that will fall

What does that imply?

Section VI: Growth

Fall

Fall is my favorite time of year

It reminds me that we all go through changes

Even nature becomes something different

It recognizes the need to shed from its past

Face Your Fear

What if you knew what steps you should take?

What if you couldn't make a mistake?

What if your path was finally clear?

What if you knew which way to steer?

What if you knew that you could not fail?

What if you knew that you would prevail?

What if you finally faced your fear?

Would all of your worries disappear?

Boundaries

You may not know this

But I believe that you should

Boundaries aren't optional

They're there for our own good

So if someone tries to tear yours down

Make sure that they're stuck

With stakes in the ground

No More Apologies

There comes a point in time

Where a person has said "sorry"

So many times

That it has lost all its meaning

And when this occurs

I know it may be hard

But break that cycle

Don't give them the chance

To be "sorry" again

Ascend

When you wonder if you will ever win

And you keep falling down, time and again

It may seem like a never-ending trend

But this is not the end—ascend

Breathe

What if you just stopped

Just stopped and caught your breath

Your breath that you've been holding

Been holding in all day

There's tension in your chest

Your chest won't decompress

Won't decompress unless

You breathe it all away

Life Is Short

Life is short

Or so I've been told

It doesn't last long

Even for the old

Eighty years, give or take

Life is really what you make

Life is precious, do not waste it

It may be hard, but you can face it

Find a way to make your time count

Instead of focusing on the amount

Perennial

I will survive

And I will bloom plentiful

I will revive

For I am perennial

Stuck Inside Your Head

I think I've cracked the code

I've finally found the key

To release me from my chains

And set my body free

I've been stuck in my mind

Sinking like a ship

But no matter what I try

I just can't get a grip

I've tried all of the meds

And I've tried all of the tricks

But nothing seems to help

Been depressed since I was six

I felt like I was stuck

In this never-ending pain

But recently I realized

A way to win the game

Depression is a devil

That feeds on you like prey

By taking all your energy

So you can't face the day

To get out of this cycle

There's something you must do

Do the things you love

And you will make it through

Depression is deceitful

And tells you just to rest

But movement is like medicine

When you are depressed

Build on your momentum

When it's hard to move

Fight against fatigue

And things will soon improve

I know it will be hard

But get out of your bed

The covers are keeping you

Stuck inside your head

On the Mend

I'm on the mend.

Up and up,

An upward trend.

But I'm still not whole.

All in all,

There's still a hole.

But I'm on the rise.

By and by,

I've dried my eyes.

I am alive.

In the end,

I will survive.

WORRY

Whenever you're worried

Or anxious or scared

Rise and

Recite that

You are prepared

Grow at Your Own Pace

Growth can happen very fast

Before time has even passed

But other times, growth is slow

And we don't have much to show

In the end, it's not a race

We all grow at our own pace

Dead Shot

When I was a barista

We had a saying

That's stuck in my mind

And keeps on replaying

"Don't let your shot die"

Was the phrase we would speak

If you let your shot die

Your coffee would be weak

The espresso would be bitter

If the shot wasn't used

Within ten seconds

Of being infused

But in that phrase

There is some wisdom

And I am here

So that I can give some

Don't let your shot die

If you're given a chance

To get ahead in life

Or simply advance

Don't give up your dreams

Or end up a quitter

If you let your shot die

You'll end up bitter

Flourish

Flaccid flower, left to die

Discarded and forgot

Flaccid flower, say goodbye

Plucked from your pot

Flaccid flower, there it lay

With its wilted stem

Flaccid flower, thrown away

Began to grow again

Start with a Simple Step

For me, finishing a task has always been easy

Getting started is the hard part

Once I do, the momentum carries me through to the finish line

But in the beginning is when I give up

Before I have even taken a single step

So in the future, before I have decided that I've already failed

I'll remember to start with a simple step

If I Never Try

I have all these fears

That are stopping me,

Like what if I try

And I don't succeed?

What if I shoot the shot

And it doesn't go in?

What if I play the game

But I still never win?

What if I make a move

And it's the wrong one?

What if I go outside

And get burnt by the sun?

What if I speak up

And I get shut down?

What if I make a mistake

And become "the talk of the town"?

What if I take a chance

And lose it all?

What if I try to leap

But I just fall?

What if I write my book

And it doesn't sell?

But if I never try,

I will always fail.

I Have What It Takes

I'm not willing to risk it all

So don't ask me to pretend like

I have what it takes

I know without a doubt that

In the end

My fear is what defines me

And that

I'll always be afraid

You can lie and tell me that

I will be brave

When danger comes my way

I am frozen by fear

Never again will I believe that

I have what it takes.

[Now read me backwards]

Journey

We're each on a journey

But along different paths

That sometimes cross

And overlap

We each have a mission

That's unique for just us

That we can accomplish

Without all the rush

The Person I've Become

Sometimes I wonder

Why my life has been so hard

But if it weren't that way

I don't think I would be the person that I've become

Endless Chances for Change

I've realized that life is a series of inevitable change—

Every day different than the last.

Perhaps we are all just trying to break free from the bindings of our past.

Might I remind you that Band-Aids don't fix bullet holes?

So we focus on the future and aim for our goals.

The world spins around us faster than ever,

And time never slows, despite our every endeavor.

At the end of the day, I often fall short—

My ball bounces far away from the court.

But there's still another game to play,

And another chance in each new day.

Section VII: Faith

Straight and Narrow

I've never quite followed

The straight and narrow

I end up lost

Like a wayward arrow

Off-trailing my way

Through an unknown path

Never once considering

The aftermath

The farther I stray

The more lost I get

But even still

I do not quit

I cut down a vine

And push past a bolder

All the while

I'm only getting older

I guess I am stubborn

And want things my way

But I make things worse

By the end of the day

If I follow my own path

It will lead to destruction

I can't make it on my own

I need some instruction

God hears my voice

And He leads me home

With Him by my side

I am never alone

Overflow

Sometimes I feel anxious

I get so caught up

In everything around me

I just can't keep up

I feel pressure that surrounds me

I feel like giving up

But Your presence grounds me

And You overflow my cup

Never Too Far Gone

I look around me and all that I see

Is each of the gifts You have given to me

From the depths of the oceans

To the tops of the trees

The vastness of heaven

And everything beneath

When I look around me

I simply can't believe

That You would do all of this

For someone like me

Like a father building a treehouse for his son

You built me the earth before my life had begun

I don't deserve it, but You give anyway

You keep giving gifts when I push you away

Each breath that I take

And every move that I make

Every morning that I awake

You work together for my sake

You gave me a home

When I felt all alone

You directed my paths

When I felt I couldn't last

When life felt impossible

You made a way

When I wasn't with you

You decided to stay

Why do You want me?

Why do You care?

Why do You seek me

When I am not there?

You have everything

But still, You want me

You mold me into the person I should be

And although I don't deserve it

You stay when times get tough

And although I make mistakes

You tell me I'm enough

You chase after me

No matter how far I've run

You don't give up on me

Until my heart is won

And then You reassure me

That I'm never too far gone

Wounded

These wounds may never heal

And I don't like the way I feel

So, Jesus, take the wheel

Because right now I can't deal

I am all alone

And I'm far from home

Please Fix Me

I feel unclean, unkept, undesirable

I feel as if my whole entity is dirty from the inside out

I have made so many mistakes and done things that I can never take back

Things I am so ashamed of

Things that I can't cover up

I feel like there is no room for repair

Like an old home that needs to be completely knocked down

Nothing at all salvageable or worth keeping

Like I am not worth the effort to put back together

Like it would be easier to just do away with me completely

I need more than just a new coat of paint

I need a complete overhaul

I don't know how to fix me

But maybe You can

Testing, Testing

Testing, Testing

1, 2, 3

Is anyone out there

Listening to me?

Testing, Testing

1, 2, 3

Can anyone out there

Hear my plea?

Be Found

Do you ever feel like no matter how fast you run,

you're stuck in the same place, when it's all said and done?

Do you ever feel like you're chasing something you will

never catch, or like a dog playing an endless game of

fetch?

Do you ever feel like a hamster on a wheel, or like your

entire body is one big Achilles' heel?

When you are sinking, but would rather be surfing…

When you can't stop thinking and your mind is bursting…

Maybe you are right where you're supposed to be,

So just stop trying so hard to flee.

Stop running and look around.

Stop trying to get lost and finally be found.

www.ingramcontent.com/pod-product-compliance
Lightning Source LLC
Chambersburg PA
CBHW052258220526
45471CB00001B/384